Understanding the Training Function

The South East Essex
College of Arts & Technology
Carnarvon Road, Southend-on-Sea, Essex SS2 6LS
Phone 0702 220400 Fax 0702 432320 Minicom 0702 220642

The Competent Trainer's Toolkit Series
by David G. Reay

This book is the first 'tool' in *The Competent Trainer's Toolkit Series*. The other titles cover the whole of the training cycle: identifying training needs and preparing a strategy; moving on through a guide to understanding how people learn, to ways of selecting methods of training, ways to implement the training and lastly, ways to evaluate training.

Understanding the Training Function stands outside the training cycle, and looks at the whole thing from a detached perspective. The other books are more focused on the individual parts of the cycle.

Understanding the Training Function

DAVID G REAY

Kogan Page Ltd, London
Nichols Publishing Company,
New Jersey

Published in association with OTSU LIMITED

First published in 1994
Reprinted in 1995

Kogan Page Limited
120 Pentonville Road
London N1 9JN

© OTSU Ltd 1994, 1995

British Library Cataloguing in Publication Data

A CIP record of this book is available from the British Library.

ISBN 0 7494 1282 8

Printed and bound in Great Britain by Biddles Ltd, Guildford and King's Lynn

Contents

Acknowledgements

This series is to a large extent based on OTSU's experiences during the past decade. Because of this, so many people have been involved in its formulation, it would be impossible to name them all. However, there are a number of people without whose help this series would not have seen the light of day.

I would like therefore to give my sincere thanks to Paul Leach for his constant support with writing, Adrian Spooner for his editing skill, Aidan Lynn for setting the series in motion, Jill Sharpe and Kathleen Gibson for design and desk-top publishing, Dorothy Reay and Amanda Froggatt for proof-reading and finally Dolores Black at Kogan Page who didn't mind flexible deadlines.

Introduction

Who this Book is For

Until quite recently, the target for this book would have been simple to define; 'trainer' or 'training manager' would have done the trick very succinctly. However, as people are seen to be contributing more and more to the success of the organization in which they work, an increasing number of people recognize that they have an important role to play in training — if not as full-time dedicated trainers, then as committed supporters of the training function.

For example, there are line managers who may be asked to guide members of their team through a specific training module, senior managers who are being asked to provide resources for training, and board members who are being asked for major investment in training. It is essential that all these people are aware of what the training function is, in order to give it the support it deserves, and this book is for them.

This series is however aimed primarily at trainers and training managers so I hope that they find this introductory book helpful in reviewing the role of training.

This book will be of direct benefit to teachers, lecturers and students in schools, colleges or other forms of further education. It is, however, aimed primarily at trainers and training managers and focuses on such key issues as the way training is perceived and its potential contribution to the quality of life of the people within an organization, as well as to the profitability of the organization itself.

Objectives

By the time you have worked through this book, you should be better able to:

- describe a variety of reasons why organizations train
- identify the reasons why your organization trains
- recognize the expectations which different individuals and groups within your organization have of training
- promote training
- describe the activities which make up training within the training cycle
- identify the training activities which are relevant to your job in your organization
- describe your role within your organization.

Overview

To help you find your way round this book, I have prepared an overview so that you can see what is contained in each chapter.

Chapter 1 — Why Organizations Train

You will see that I have divided the reasons why organizations train into two broad headings: business and people reasons. Under each of these headings there are several items, and you'll be able to examine each of them in turn. You'll be able to assess your organization's reasons for training — an essential prerequisite for successful development.

Chapter 2 — Why Groups and Individuals Train

This chapter could be subtitled 'What do people expect from training?'. It explores common conceptions and misconceptions of what training is all about and then shows you ways in which you can raise people's expectations of training. You will see that high expectations are another essential prerequisite for successful training. This chapter also explains the merits of reactive and proactive training and you'll see for yourself the circumstances in which it is a very good idea to take the initiative with training.

Chapter 3 — Promoting Training

Chapter 3 shows you training as a product which has customers, a market, selling-points — and all the other features of a merchantable product. Of course, knowing that your training provision is a product will mean that you'll have to sell it, and Chapter 3 outlines key elements in a successful training sales strategy.

Chapter 4 — The Training Function — What is it?

This chapter examines the relationship between the training function and the host organization. Once you've seen what makes a good relationship and how to realign the training function if it is at all marginalized, you'll see that training involves gathering intelligence, making appropriate responses, identifying gaps and deciding whether and how to fill those gaps. Only at this stage do the more visible elements of the training function come out: planning, running and evaluating training materials and courses for people.

Chapter 5 — The Trainer's Role

The role of the trainer is divided into six task areas, and the tasks in each area are examined. By the end of this chapter, you will be able to identify in which area or areas most of your tasks lie, so that you will be able to identify and describe your own role within the organization.

How to Use this Book

This is not a text which you will read once and then put away never to read again (I hope!). Its inclusion in the *Competent Trainer's Toolkit* series indicates that it is designed for you to use in your work as a trainer.

How you work through the book is really up to you. You may, if you wish, work through the pages in order from front to back and cover the whole text in that way. The book is constructed logically so that you can work right through it. Alternatively you can dip into a chapter at a time, as and when you need to.

There is a range of activities and assignments for you to complete inside each chapter. Activities are distinguished by the fact that there is some feedback — not always in the form of right or wrong answers, because there are not always hard-and-fast right or wrong answers to be had.

Assignments, on the other hand, are an opportunity for you to get out into your organization and ask some of the questions which will help you to analyse your own situation and your own needs. It would be misleading of us to include answers but where appropriate I have made comments based on my own organization's experiences with a variety of clients. However, you should bear in mind when reading these that your situation is bound to have its own unique features.

Completing the activities and assignments provides you with an additional benefit. By doing these you will be creating a body of evidence for your vocational qualification, and if you wish to follow that route you should keep this text and the outcomes of the activities and assignments as a record of your study. Because the book calls on you to write your own thoughts and think about your own situation it will become your personal record and guide to your understanding of the training function.

You should feel free to write notes at any point in the margins or on the text. In fact, the more notes you write, the more useful this book will be to you in the long run.

Training and Development Lead Body Competences

A Brief Summary

Many trainers and training managers in the UK are actively seeking professional vocational qualifications, through the growing National Vocational Qualification route. This book and series can help you to achieve them. There are competences at level 3 and level 4 of the NVQ in Training and Development for which you will be able to use this book as part of your portfolio of evidence.

To make it easier for you to include the assignments in this book in your portfolio of evidence, I have prepared, on the following page, a matrix which matches a list of assignments which appear in this book and the competences, published in autumn 1994, which appear in the scheme booklets provided by the awarding bodies. Simply tick off the numbered assignments as you do them. Then, when you've completed this book, you can include the book itself together with any supporting documents you may create as you work through it in your NVQ portfolio. This simple matching technique will allow your NVQ assessor easily to locate your evidence and match it against the relevant criteria.

While no one assignment fulfils a whole element of competence, each assignment goes towards meeting performance criteria outlined in the elements shown. It follows that this book will make a signficant contribution to your portfolio as a whole. Other books in this series will match other criteria in the TDLB list of elements.

Assignment at end of Chapter	The Assignment Counts as Evidence Towards these Elements								
1	B211	E123	E413						
2	A211	A212	D113	D211					
3	B221	B222	E221	E222	E223	E412			
4	A211	E421	E422						
5	E411	E412							

A211   Collect information from individuals on their learning requirements
A212   Identify and agree individuals' learning requirements
B211   Select option for meeting learning requirements
B221   Identify options for training and development sessions
B222   Design training and development session for learners
D113   Review progress with learners
D211   Collect information from individuals for non-competence based assessment
E123   Introduce improvements to training and development in an organisation
E221   Identify potential improvements to training and development programmes
E222   Plan the introduction of improvements to training and development programmes
E223   Implement improvements to training and development programmes
E411   Research ways in which people learn
E412   Develop training and development methods to support different learning styles
E413   Test and modify proposed training and development methods
E421   Identify new approaches for training and development
E422   Generate new approaches to training and development

So What is Training About?

Over the years I have been privileged to visit many organizations in Europe and North America. As a result I've had many opportunities to talk about training and education with people at all levels within a wide variety of industrial, commercial and government sectors. When I ask 'What does "training" mean to you?' I never know what answers to expect. Here are just some of the answers I've encountered:

- · 'Training helped me get where I am today'
- · 'Training was really useful — I learnt how to do my job'
- · 'Everything you do is a sort of training, because you're always learning'
- · 'Training's got very little to do with the real world, I'm afraid'
- · 'If you're selected for training, you know you're on the way up'
- · 'If you crash out you'll generally get training — but it's probably too late!'
- · 'Training costs us too much money and I doubt it does us any good!'
- · 'I can't remember!'

These and other comments are pronounced with every possible shade of nuance from the heavily ironic and discontented to the genuinely enthusiastic and committed. Unfortunately, comments like these don't lead you to any satisfactory definition of what training is — save to say that it is all things to all people. Just as people's opinion about a certain model of car is determined by their most recent experiences of it, so their idea of what training is seems often to be coloured by what they feel training has most recently done for them.

So What Should Training be About?

There has long been a tension between training and education and although this is not the place to go into depth about the issue I would like to comment briefly on it to help set the position of both this book and the rest of the series. The difference between training and education can be summarized thus: 'Education is about the emancipation of the mind. Training is about learning a skill'. I take the view that learning a skill **can be** as emancipating to the mind as discovering Plato but only if the training experience is designed to be so.

So what should training be about? I take the view that training should be about enabling an organization to achieve its aims. But it will only do that by enabling the people within that organization. If the outcomes of training cannot be seen to achieve both of these targets, then one must question the wisdom of putting any resource whatever into it.

Equally, I take the view that all good training includes elements of both 'education' and 'training'.

What Training Does

It is ultimately more useful to focus on the notion of what training does for people and for organizations that what it is. It should be the outcomes of training which justify its existence within any organization. With my mind fixed on the outcomes of training, then, I propose the following operational definition of 'training' which will underpin this whole book.

- Training is a collection of actions, which enables the organization to achieve its goals through enabling, empowering and developing to its fullest, the potential of the individuals within that organization.

You will notice that my proposed definition centres on the people within an organization and focuses on ways of liberating the potential resource that they bring to the business. This book rest on that definition. By the time you have read through this book and have responded to the practical and professional challenges it will make of you, I believe that you will be in a better position to question, support or alter my operational definition — and be in a much better position to analyse your current role in training, and design and justify what you future role in training should be.

Why Organizations Train

Organizations train for a variety of reasons.

Take a few moments now and write down three reasons why your organization provides training — if it doesn't provide training write down three reasons why it **should**!

Three reasons why my organization trains or should train are:

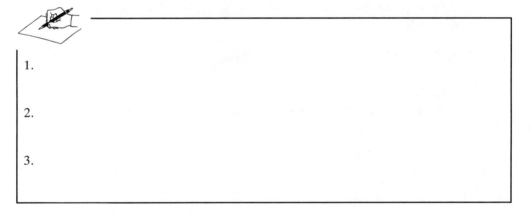

1.

2.

3.

We will come back to your comments a little later but before we do we have created two pen-pictures of very different organizations for you to analyse in terms of the possible results different organizations are seeking as they train.

Below are descriptions of activities of Every Day Ltd and Barker, Smith & Newton.

1.   Every Day Ltd

Every Day Ltd is the brainchild of F R Days. The company employs 30 people and they provide tailor-made diaries for large organizations.

The diaries contain all the information which is important for the client organization during the year, and they provide time-plans and deadlines so that:

- figures can be rounded up in time for the accounting period deadlines
- targets can be met in time for the various reporting days
- letters can be written to clients before the tax-year end — or whatever internal milestones the client organization passes year by year.

The diaries have become popular with the client organizations and F R Days is always looking for new information to put in them. One company wants staff appraisal information to be included in the diary so that individuals can record their personal targets and literally carry them round with them all day and make a note of their achievements.

Of the 30 people working for Every Day there are, apart from F R Days himself:

- a marketer
- a team of focus researchers and analysts
- a team of three writers
- three designers
- six page layout operatives
- two printers
- five support staff, who drive, collect, deliver and distribute materials
- five administrative staff.

And they're all busy all the time, as deadlines become shorter and shorter.

In common with many small businesses, staff turnover is high as a percentage of the work-force — up to eight people may leave in a period of 12 months. However, despite this, morale in the business is high.

Cont/d . . .

At times when a job or two is vacant, the deadlines imposed by clients become a problem.

The business continues to grow and prosper and has attracted favourable comment in trade magazines.

However, there is the threat of two other organizations now setting up similar ventures.

People from some client organizations drop broad hints that they'd like to work for F R Days.

2.   Barker, Smith & Newton (BSN)

BSN is a large concern with 10,000 employees in three small town locations across the country.

From humble origins as a timber supplier in 1906 it now manufactures all sorts of goods, but specializes in furniture which it delivers to out of town outlets.

Because of the way the company grew there is a strong tradition of sons and more recently daughters following parents into the business.

Five years ago the company suffered a major labour relations trauma and the result was a lasting rift between shop-floor workers and management. Since then mistakes leading to reworking and accidents have both increased.

BSN is aware that the competition in the marketplace is operating with increased mechanization. BSN has responded quickly by buying new equipment. However there is strong resistance to its use among the workforce.

The company needs to bring in expertise from the outside, but such is its reputation that quality staff just can't be tempted to apply for the jobs.

Morale in the business is low and the press has got wind of it. A climate of gloom prevails.

Reasons for Training

Write in the box below three reasons why you think (a) Every Day and (b) Barker, Smith & Newton should train.

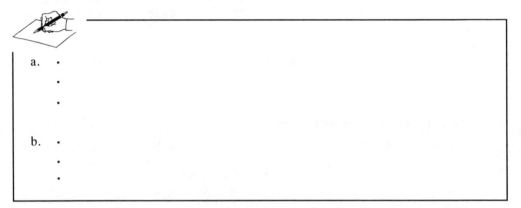

a. •

   •

   •

b. •

   •

   •

Your answers may be vague or specific, but will probably be in tune with these:

For Every Day, training will enable the business to:

- grow and develop
- ensure new arrivals are successfully inducted
- ensure the current success continues

For BSN, training could:

- change attitudes
- improve morale
- reduce reworking

It will help you to understand the training function if you spend some time analysing the reasons why these organizations need to train. Your analysis should consider the situation from two perspectives; the **business** perspective and the **people** perspective.

The Business Perspective

Both organizations have business problems.

For Every Day there is a high staff turnover leading to problems in maintaining quality and there is the threat of increased competition which makes the need for greater efficiency paramount. BSN faces the threat of more efficient companies putting it out of business, but its more recent history and traditional workforce is making change problematic.

Both organizations need now to look at how training might play a part in helping them to solve their problems and meet their business aims of survival and growth. From the business perspective, training needs to achieve the following in each case:

a.   At Every Day, training needs to:

   - reduce staff turnover
   - improve product quality
   - free up more time for ideas to be developed to help offset the threat of competition
   - increase response time
   - improve the levels of value added activity within the business
   - increase competitiveness
   - push the cost-base down.

b.   For BSN, training needs to:

   - ensure maximum efficiency in use of the new plant and equipment
   - improve the company's external image
   - reduce costs by eliminating both accidents and mistakes which require reworking
   - improve the levels of value added activity within the business
   - increase competitiveness
   - push the cost-base down.

Training is not the only way to achieve these ends. Investment in plant and infrastructure, employment of new personnel or devising improved systems could also contribute. None the less, improving the skills people apply to their work would be an important — probably the most important — element in any package of measures applied to address the business needs.

The People Perspective

It is important to realize that training can only impact on the business needs if it impacts effectively on the people in the business. It follows that you can look at training primarily in terms of the impact it has on people, and then go on to see how this has an indirect but none the less substantial effect on the bottom line.

In people terms, therefore, training could benefit our companies in the following ways:

a.   at Every Day, training could lead to:

- increased motivation and commitment
- improved skill levels
- multi-skilled staff
- more internal candidates for promotion.

b.   at BSN, which is suffering from the detrimental effects of poor labour relations and a traditional workforce who are resistant to change, training could lead to:

- improved morale
- improved skill levels
- people being encouraged to feel valued and important to the organization
- improved level of commitment
- raised confidence
- increased knowledgeability.

In practice it is impossible to separate out these two perspectives on training. In the experience of my team those organizations which have achieved the most thorough training have actively sought to develop their people **and** benefit the business, and this view will surface several times in the course of the rest of this book.

The ultimate aim of training must always be the survival and prosperity of the organization, however. To take our two companies:

Every Day should train to build on their growth and continue their improvement. BSN should train to reverse their decline and stop the rot.

Now go back to the comments you noted on page 18 about why **your** organization provides training.

Re-read them and extend them, putting a people perspective and a business perspective on each one.

1.

2.

3.

The next step is to take these ideas a stage further by finding out from others in your organization why your company bothers with training — or if it doesn't, why not and why it should.

The information you collect here will be useful when you come to the design stage later.

Select three key people, and list them below. Then gather them together and ask them why your organization provides training (or should).

Name	Why we provide training (or should)

You should also note down whether these individuals put a people perspective or a business perspective on their reasons.

The Benefits of Training

The next step is to identify, not why we train but what benefits come from training. I said earlier that it is the outcomes of training which are the key to its utility. In our experience there are direct benefits, which are clearly measurable against predetermined criteria. Benefits such as improved performance or increased materials throughput might count as 'direct benefits'.

There are also 'indirect benefits' — such as the effect your well-trained workforce has on potential clients. These are difficult to measure, but none the less real for that.

So what benefits do key people in your organization expect from training? Direct? Indirect? A mixture of both? And what specific benefits do they mention?

It will be more useful if you ask these questions of the people who know the answers and since you're dealing with matters of policy, the people with the answers are likely to be senior figures in the hierarchy.

Assignment:

On a separate piece of paper create a list of people and their positions within your organization who will be able to give you information about the benefits they expect from training.

When you talk to the policy-makers in your organization, exactly what questions would you ask them? Use the space below to sketch out some questions which develop the theme of benefits from training.

Our thoughts are as follows:

- start by asking what training they are aware of taking place. How much does it cost the business?
- ask if they consider that the training is delivering any benefits. Move on to probe areas where the organization needs to see greater benefits
- ask what role training might have in achieving these benefits
- find out how the expected benefits tie in to your organization's mission, values and objectives.

Of course, our thoughts as outlined above may not be appropriate to your situation. Some organizations brief their trainers very thoroughly and have available 'policy statements' or 'mission statements for trainers' which outline very thoroughly exactly what is required and expected in terms of the training department's contribution. In such cases, an interview with a senior manager may be irrelevant. If it takes place at all it will just be to confirm that the printed policy is relevant and current.

Other organizations may have a training policy statement which is poorly thought through, or so bland as to be meaningless. In these cases, your job as trainer is to use interviews to firm up your policy. The point is that to understand the training function you have to understand that it has a job to do — a specific, measurable and achievable job. Only when you've determined what training benefits are expected and required will you be able to set your sights on where you're going.

Use the box on the next page to write down what the key people in your organization are looking for in the way of benefits from training. Then compare your findings to the results of our enquiries over the years, which appear on the following pages.

The kind of benefits key people in my organization would like to see from training are:

On the next page are some of the more common benefits which organizations expect:

Staff Who are More Efficient

The link between efficiency and training is very clear in the case of organizations whose people need to learn how to work to new systems and procedures if they are to be as efficient as their competitors. Increased efficiency usually leads directly to greater profit, and staff are freed up to develop new ideas.

Staff Who are More Knowledgeable

Not only do salespeople need to know what their team of producers can make, but also at what cost, and in how much time. And producers need to know what the client needs. Recent changes in business operations, such as the advent of total quality, have made clear that employees' knowledge of other employees' tasks has a direct bearing on motivation. People need a wider range of knowledge than ever before. This range involves, the business, its markets, its products, their role, contribution and responsibilities.

Staff Who are More Confident

The confidence of any company's staff is reflected in the continual improvement the business makes. Confident staff are predisposed to pushing back the boundaries.

Quality Service

The word 'quality' is notoriously difficult to define, but all organizations are seeking to provide what the customer needs:

- on time, every time
- within budget
- accurately.

Increased Profitability

The 'bottom line' is what it's all about. Profitable businesses create employment and generate wealth for the community and for society as a whole. Unprofitable ones don't.

Increased profitability is closely linked to the amount of value-added activity which takes place within an organization, and training has a key role to play in ensuring that adding-value is at its maximum.

Increased Competitiveness

Most organizations have within their people enough knowledge, expertise and resourcefulness to improve their competitiveness by their own efforts.

However it is my experience that this ability, expertise and resourcefulness lie dormant. The training function is the logical diviner and developer of these abilities.

Good Training Implies a Good Employer

You'll hear it said that training is an investment in people, and the logic of the statement is inescapable. Training does enable people to acquire the knowledge and skills they need to earn a living — and to improve their standard of living. And that knowledge and these skills can not be taken back from them. Some would say that means that as soon as they get them they'll leave.

That's part of the double-edged sword of training, but if people leave because they're now better trained there's likely to be a much stronger underlying reason why they want to move.

People Feel Good About Working There

In a survey carried out among the Fortune 500 companies in the USA, most people put training above pay in their top ten reasons for coming to work. Industrial Society results in the UK have supported the Fortune 500 findings.

It follows that if you train well, your people are more likely to be motivated.

And from that it follows that the quality of the work produced is more likely to be high.

Customers Like the Feel of the Organization

At first glance it may seem odd that a well-trained organization should 'feel better' than a poorly trained or untrained one.

On reflection, however the following features are all symptomatic of a 'bad atmosphere' and of a lack of training:

- low morale
- recriminations
- mutual blame
- avoidance of responsibility
  and
- fear.

People who don't know what they're doing will always feel uncomfortable and will always communicate this to their customers.

An organization in which people do know what they're doing and do it, will always feel more comfortable to a customer.

When a customer comes to the business, they'll get what they want, on time, every time, at the right price. They'll expect the best, and they'll get it.

But how do you make sure customers get what they expect?
You guessed it — train your people to meet customer expectations.

And when those expectations are raised — and not disappointed, of course — then your organization will be able to reap the rewards which are associated with a good reputation for quality service and products.

Employees Like the Feel of the Organization

Good training can have a positive effect not only on your organization's customers — but on the employees themselves. Consider these two situations and your reaction to them.

Situation A

Imagine for a moment that you have just been told that from tomorrow morning you are in charge of the Byzantine Footstool Manufacturing Plant (having previously been the only member of the Hole Punching and Paper Clip Bending Department). You will then be in charge of 232 people and have to make sure they meet the target of 650 footstools per week, on pain of death.

How do you feel?

Situation B

Now imagine you've just been told that in three months' time you'll be taking over the Byzantine Footstool Manufacturing Plant. During the first month you'll go on a full-time course, during the second you'll work in each section of the plant for a few days, and during the third you'll divide your time 50/50 between attending another course and working directly with the current manager.

Now how do you feel?

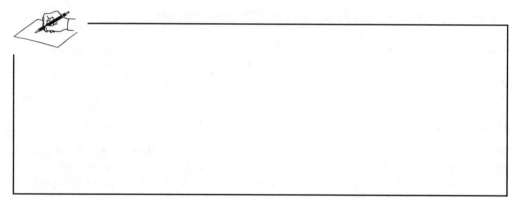

In providing feedback for that activity, we are in a privileged position. We've been talking to people in situations of types A and B for years, and this is what they feel.

Type A — (no training) — employees feel:

- threatened
- inadequate
- resentful
- stressed
- fearful.

You'll agree that a workforce with this potent mix of perceptions and emotions isn't going to be inclined to produce good work.

Type B — (successful training) — employees feel:

- confident
- relaxed
- keen to learn the new skills
- able to voice their concerns.

Just the sort of people you need to have on your side in challenging times such as those presented by today's economic climate.

The point about the benefits of training is this: the specific objective of any individual piece of training is not the only thing which that training achieves. Each piece should contribute to an overall 'training-orientated' ethos.

It is impossible to say how much each individual piece of training contributes, but the cumulative benefit can be enormous, if there is consistency throughout.

Indicators of Training Benefits

I'd like to finish off this chapter with a view of the indicators you can expect to see in your organization to show you that the benefits are beginning to accrue. First and foremost you might think of the bottom line, and, true enough: costs will fall and income will rise. But you should look more closely:

What would you look for to corroborate your 'hunch' that your reduced costs and increased income are indeed training-related?

Thinking first of your current employees, and then of your future, potential employees, consider what might be the symptoms you would look for to indicate that benefits from training are beginning to show.

> I will look for these signs of benefits in our staff:
>
> •
> •
> •
> •

We can't know exactly what you wrote there, or how many benefits you expect to find. We're sure however, you'll be interested to compare your thoughts to our experiences.

Current Staff will Stay Longer

The feelings of confidence, competence and well-being in a good training organization tempt people to stay. They know that whatever changes may occur, they'll be given what they need to cope. Moving out of your organization is a step into the unknown.

Less Sickness and Absence

It's there! Your staff will actually be healthier. The stress levels associated with fear and feelings of inadequacy are very high, and so affect people's health. The reduction of stress brought about by successful training improves their health.

People who might have been tempted to feign illness rather than face an impossible situation will tend to be ready to accept the challenge if they know they can tackle it.

Also, people who are valued and respected repay that treatment in kind. They are more productive, the quality of their work is higher, and they will get a genuine buzz from coming to work and doing a good job.

We must stress that we are realists. There will always be people who are genuinely ill — and there will always be malingerers. Training will not help these people directly, but it will allow you to identify who they are and take appropriate action.

Staff Will Show More Willingness

Trained staff who know the business will be more likely to respond to urgent requests for co-operation — because they know why. Also, organizations which train are making a positive statement about the value they put on their people, and people are less likely to behave antagonistically towards each other in such organizations.

You Will Find Greater Staff Loyalty

We can provide an example of what we mean. A large organization with a poor reputation for training always had a ready supply of employees who would write to the press — anonymously of course — about 'management excesses'.

Three years and a major training initiative later and **another** critical letter appeared in the press. This time however, the editor was inundated with indignant letters from employees who **knew** what the situation was and were able and willing to set the record straight.

It Will Be Easier to Attract Staff

People know which organizations provide training and which don't, particularly people within a given industrial sector. If you can't offer quality training, you're less likely to attract quality applicants.

Summary

Chapter 1 of this book has dealt with the reasons why organizations train. You read first of all that their reasons for training have to be viewed from the **business** perspective and the **people** perspective. Taking the business perspective, training has a direct and measurable effect on business performance in money terms. We singled out the following as good examples of reasons for training seen from the business angle:

- more efficient staff
- reduced costs
- better customer service
- fewer accidents
- increased competitiveness.

We then moved on to show you the reasons for training viewed from the people perspective.

These included:

- increased motivation and commitment
- improved skill level
- more internal candidates for promotion
- improved morale
- increased confidence
- increased knowledgeability.

There then followed an examination of the benefits organizations expect from training, including:

- raised customer expectations of service levels
- raised staff expectations of the organization
- raised customer satisfaction levels. Customers will speak of your organization as one which gets things **right** — every time

- staff who are more loyal, flexible and co-operative.

Lastly, you saw a list of indicators which show you that the increased success in your organization is genuinely attributable to training:

- increased loyalty
- decreased sickness
- greater success in attracting quality staff.

Before you leave this section, we recommend you complete three assignments which will encourage you to think about why your organization trains.

Assignment 1: Staff Turnover

Select four job titles from your organization. For example they could be from the categories of skilled, unskilled, clerical and management. Then find out how many people there are with the different titles you've selected. Find out how many left those positions over the last year. Calculate the percentage which is known as 'labour turnover'.

How does this percentage compare with the industry average? If your organization says it provides job security, a career, and support for its staff, then you would expect your percentage to be below the labour turnover average for your industry.

If not:

- *are salaries too low?*
- *are there too few promotion opportunities?*

Training can't address these points directly. But —

- *are managers motivating their teams?*
- *is induction training satisfactory?*
- *are people receiving the training they really need for their jobs?*

If not — you have uncovered a training need.

Assignment 2: Recruitment

Is there one category of staff — managers, perhaps, or technicians — which your organization is having to recruit from outside? Find out the figures for the past year. If one or more categories stand out then you have identified a possible opportunity for training to play a key role in the future development of the business. You could find it necessary to develop existing staff in these areas.

Assignment 3: Customer Satisfaction

Does your organization keep a record of customer complaints — and are they regularly analysed? If the answer is 'No', your organization may be less concerned about its external image than is healthy.

If you can refer to this kind of analysis, find out how many complaints relate to product or process, and how many to people. Try to identify the tone of the complaints — are they written in sorrow or in anger?

What is the underlying message of the complaint? Are people surprised at having to complain, or do they see a complaint as the only way of gaining satisfaction?

If you have no access to this kind of information, try imagining you are a customer. Describe your organization from the customer's point of view.

You could also ask your colleagues to describe 'customers' in a maximum of three words.

The answers to these questions should tell you how well your organization is developing a team of people who are keen and able to offer a high standard of service. If it is not doing this very well, you have a training problem.

Why Groups and Individuals Train

If you ask people in an organization why they bother to take training, you tend to get two basic responses:

- because they want to

  or

- because they have to.

Then there is the third response:

- they would train if they could — but they can't, because no training is available.

Once you have found out if people in your organization fall into the 'want to', 'have to' or 'can't' category there are other key issues to be addressed. Issues like:

- why do they fall into these categories?
- how do they find out?

and once you've got the information you need to ask:

- what can the training function do about it?

This chapter will address these questions, and suggest ways in which you can answer them for your organization.

'Want to', 'Have to' — or 'Can't'

The question of whether people can or cannot train in an organization has to be dealt with first, because if there has been no training in your organization (or at least none for certain groups and individuals) then the question of why they **have** trained is irrelevant.

Finding the gap between training provision and the perceived need for training is a key early task for the new trainer.

Assignment:

1. *Ask line managers whether they have tried to get people on to courses and failed.*
2. *Ask trainers (or consult the records) about the rate of take-up on training courses which have been an offer.*

The result of this investigation will show you whether you are in a situation where:

- there is excess training provision, or
- there is inadequate provision, or
- there is the correct amount of training provision.

Of these three situations, the first two are the most problematical to the trainer.

Excess training provision implies that the people in the organization do not want what the training function is offering. We will help you to explore this more in Chapter 3, on promoting training.

Inadequate training provision implies that the people want more than they can get. Your people may see training as available only to the few or as elitist.

However, even a perception that there is the correct amount of training provided is no cause for long-term comfort. That perception needs to be checked as does the relationship between the training and the organization's mission and objectives.

People are likely to see the training function as 'unable to deliver', and this will lead to disenchantment and frustration.

The point is that we live in an era where people's expectations of training are very high. For example, they see competitors in the Far East offering successful training to their employees, and building up their business as they do so.

If you fail to deliver for any reason, you are quite likely to antagonize your people.

So, back to the first two points raised at the start of the chapter.

'Having to' Train Rather Than 'Wanting to' Train

I'm sure that as a trainer you will have come across (or will definitely do so in the future) this sort of comment from trainees when you ask them why they're training:

- 'My manager sends us all every two years'
- 'I can't get my licence unless I go through this'
- 'I have no choice'.

What is it about training courses which makes people react in this way? All we're looking for is one simple sentence.

The simple answer is that the people are not getting the benefits they need from the courses they're attending. The chances are that the courses don't give them what they really need.

The consequence of this is that eventually people will be reluctant to attend the courses and will fail to achieve their full potential. There's a good chance that managers will stop sending people on these courses. There's also a great danger that the training function will end up completely divorced from the people it is supposed to help.

The reasons why people don't get the benefit they are supposed to from training courses are two-fold. Below is a list of comments made by people who attended training courses 'because they had to'.

- we just don't meet that sort of situation any more
- it's boring
- it keeps me away from where I need to be — at work!
- the new computer system makes what we learnt redundant
- I needed to know about next year's changes — not the current changes
- I want a proper qualification!

See if you can identify two separate main reasons why the courses failed these people.

The two basic reasons for dissatisfaction are:

1.

2.

The two main reasons are:

- the training is out of touch with reality
- the training methods are inappropriate.

So as a starting point in collecting information . . .

Get in Touch With Reality

Getting in touch with reality means having an up-to-date picture of what people need to do in your organization and the way they need to do it: in other words, skills and attitudes needed.

One reality of the modern world is the movement towards nationally recognized, transferable qualifications. This move follows the belief that people have a right to expect that training will provide them with the necessary:

- skills
- attitudes

    and

- qualifications.

But you must first take stock of your current situation before you rush out and redesign your organization's training provision. After all, it could be that all or part of your training is already providing what your people need and have come to expect. There is no point in re-inventing something which is working perfectly well.

The simplest method of finding out just how 'in touch with reality' your department is, is to ask questions. You'll see later that we recommend a questionnaire in the first instance to focus on this issue. But that same questionnaire can deal with our second point — appropriateness of training methods — at the same time.

Appropriateness of Training Methods

In our travels we have seen training methods both appropriate and inappropriate for a wide range of reasons. We have seen familiarity with computer keyboards taught using chalk and a blackboard. We've seen interviewing skills practised on CBT (computer based training). We've seen busy executives removed from their desks for days on end to study material which could have been made into a simple open learning text.

So — whereabouts in the spectrum of appropriateness does your training methodology stand?

As we said earlier, to answer the question, find out from the people who really know — the trainees who have been through the courses.

One of the most effective ways of doing this is with a well designed questionnaire. The questionnaire will ask questions which sharply focus the respondent's mind on the issues of relevance and method and, at the end of it, you'll get a good idea of:

·   where you stand

·   which areas you need to improve in.

Assignment:

Prepare a short questionnaire and distribute it to a sample of your organization's people who have been through training in your department over the last two years.

You should phrase the questions in your own way, but arrange the answers to be put on a scale of 1 to 5 so that the people:

• *can answer quickly*

• *can not 'hedge their bets' by guessing in the middle.*

Here's an example of what we mean.
On a scale of 1 to 5, where 1 is low and 5 high, how do you rate the relevance of the training you have received over the last two years?

Totally Irrelevant   Totally Relevant

1	2	3	4	5

You should develop other questions to ask about:

• *the style of the training (totally inappropriate/totally appropriate)*

• *to what extent the training was interesting or boring (completely boring/completely interesting)*

• *to what extent the training has benefited:*
  — *their careers*
  — *their relationship with customers*
  — *their relationship with colleagues.*

• *to what extent the training has improved their ability to do the job they do now.*

You should also allow a limited amount of space for respondents to make 'any further comments about what you would like training to do for you'.

Summary So Far

As always, when you're in the initial stages of finding out what training does for people, you are likely to need to ask more questions. So before we go on, let's take a look back.

First, you categorized people under three broad headings. Those who:

- take part in training because they want to
- take part in training because they have to
- would undertake training but can't, because there isn't any.

You then set out to analyse whether your organization allows everyone who wants to train to do so.

Your next step was to analyse whether your people fall largely into the 'want to' category, or the 'have to' category.

You then moved on to find out about the overall import of the training provided. Only you can know what you've learnt in your situation. Perhaps your training has been right on the button and delivered in the most appropriate way. All your people apart from a cynical minority will be in the 'want to train' group.

Perhaps your training has missed the mark completely and is delivered inappropriately. Or — and this is most likely — there's a mix. You're getting conflicting signals. Some combinations of training and trainees are working well and others aren't.

More questions will come welling up straight away. These questions could include:

- How do I improve the poor areas?
- What do people need to be trained in?
- How can I prioritize so that a finite training budget can best meet the needs of the people in the organization?

In one sentence: **what can the training function do about it?**

So on to . . .

What the Training Function Can Do About It

Assuming a situation where the people in an organization are less than satisfied with the training they receive, the training function has several options, all of them tempting, but only one of them viable. In the simplest terms, the options are:

- do nothing, change nothing, keep a low profile
- seize the initiative, change everything
- study the context further, create a strategy.

Which of these options would you choose for your situation — and why?

Here are our thoughts on the situation.

Option 1 — Do Nothing, Change Nothing

Trainers — particularly those new to an organization or to the training function — feel comfortable with this option because 'it gives them a chance to settle in and find their feet'.

Philosophically, it can be argued that every organization gets the training function it deserves, and that the position of the training function is one of being influenced rather than influencing.

We must counsel against this soft option because it is the route to stagnation. Just to repeat the courses offered last year — but this time to different people — is to fail in your duty to give people what they need.

The fact that they've had a three-day development course after two years with the business, coupled with the fact that the business is still trading does not lead logically to the conclusion that the course — or any other course — is effective.

Option 2 — Take the Initiative, Change Everything

Training has a role in every organization, but that role is not the major, leading role. You can't decide that process x needs skills y and attitudes z in the team, because only the team members know that — and only after they consider the business needs and their targets.

Some people enjoy being seen to be dynamic, and there are occasions when energy and forcefulness will stand you in good stead as a trainer. But not every occasion. Training is an ongoing job. If training were a one-off task then a sudden spurt of energy and the rapid implication of a radically new idea might be effective.

We expect our military leaders to be like this: to go in, appraise the situation, accomplish the task and get out. And quickly. But what works in a war-zone is unlikely to work for training.

Our trainers are faced with an ongoing situation. There will always be a need for training, not because you keep having to repeat things over and over when people don't learn and don't improve, but because when people learn and improve they develop new needs and newer, higher expectations than they had before, and so on ad infinitum.

Such a task is not suited to hasty action.

Option 3 — Study the Context Further, Create a Strategy

The training function exists wholly within the organization it serves. The activities it carries on would, by and large, be inappropriate in the public market place. Although the skills and attitudes it provides access to could serve people in all areas of their lives and throughout their careers, the main focus of the training function should, arguably, be the need of the organization.

Thus you see the importance of studying the context. The people within the organization **are** the organization, and you need to know the following in order to provide an appropriate training response:

- what is on their mind
- what troubles them
- what motivates them
- what they need to know

  and

- what they need to be able to do.

Being stubbornly practical people, you will want more detail than that. All we've told you is that if you want to meet the training needs of the people in your organization, you have to study the context further and create a strategy, before you do anything else.

But what does that mean in practical terms? Quite simply, it's a matter of asking questions. No matter which way your organization is structured, you'll find there are four main business activities.

Traditionally the four main business activities are covered by:

- Finance
- Marketing
- Operations
- Personnel (Human Resource Development).

In each of these areas there are key questions for you to ask — questions which will reveal to you why the people in those areas will want to train.

We'll come onto the key questions themselves in a moment, but first we need to give you a word of advice about where to find those business activities in your organization.

Some organizations are situated along departmental or functional lines. You'll find all the finance people in one or two departments, the marketers in another, and operators in one or more others, and so on. Responsibility for personnel — training, welfare, employment registration, etc is hived off under a separate roof as well. Asking your key questions will be quite easy in these circumstances. You know where to go.

Some organizations are structured along process lines. The process — be it manufacturing a tank or producing a book — is the thing; it will have its own team of dedicated people drawn from different areas of the business. The 'departments' have no independent existence except as resource banks for the process. In such organizations your key questions will need to be asked in every process team, because every process team contains all four main business activities.

Assignment: Ask the people

Go out into your organization and ask the people these questions. As we said earlier, you need to address all four business activities during your inquiries. We have provided some example questions. Be prepared to add your own or remove some of ours if you find they're irrelevant.

Cont/d . . .

Finance Questions
Is the organization growing or contracting?
Is the business becoming more or less profitable?
Is training seen as a cost or an investment?
How much money is available to spend on training?

Marketing Questions
Which market are you operating in?
What changes are taking place in each market?
Are you planning to move into new markets? Which?
What are your strengths and weaknesses compared to capabilities?
What level of service are we/should we be getting?

Operations Questions
Is the current workflow efficient?
What new methods, procedures and approaches are planned?
What will be the input of new technology?
Who will be responsible for introducing change?
What training will this change require?
What are internal communications like within your organization?

Personnel Questions
What is the typical background of staff members?
Where have your present managers come from?
Are they currently good enough to meet the challenges of the future?
If not:
    What changes will be needed?
    Will you need more staff?
    What training will you need?
    What can training contribute to making change successful?

We advised you to look at the context and then create a strategy. The context, in the light of the answers to those questions you've been asking, should be becoming clearer, and now you should be better able to create a strategy.

To return to the start of this section. You have the information. Now what is the training function going to do about it? The answer depends on your situation.

Situation 1: The Organization has Given you Carte-blanche to Determine What Happens

In this extreme but very attractive situation your role will be entirely pro-active. You will be able to say who needs what training and when and why. You may even be able to say when expertise needs to be brought in, in the form of new staff.

Case Study

Laxon's Ltd, a supplier of building materials to the construction industry was plagued by inaccurate order-filling, excess stock, poor staff attendance and high staff turnover. The new trainer analysed the situation, asked for carte-blanche and got it.

She arranged for the chairman to launch a new training initiative. The new strategy was focused on communications. The idea of holding training sessions which would be attended by their own staff together with the staff of the business which supplied Laxon's with raw materials was introduced. Later this was extended to Laxon's customers as well, so that eventually everyone throughout the supply chain knew what was needed, and what everyone's expectations and roles should be.

Errors declined, a major move towards Just-In-Time was instigated for many lines of stock, staff became happier and their expertise stayed with the company longer.

This initiative came from the training function. Because the trainer found out what the people wanted, she was able to meet their needs and give them the benefits they required.

Situation 2: The Organization Tells You What to Do

Many trainers find that their schedule for the year is mapped out for them and their own perceptions of what needs to be done aren't always asked for or acted upon.

Case Study

> An investment group was losing so many junior employees to its competitors that the trainer was asked to beef-up the induction course. The group's perception was that the juniors were frustrated by their inability to move on to important projects quickly enough after joining the business.
>
> The trainer did as requested and staff turnover at junior level did drop slightly.

Situation 3 — Bits of Both 1 and 2

This is the most common situation for new trainers to find themselves in. It's a situation where trainers are given their head in some areas, but have to follow the organization's edicts in others.

Although not ideal we reckon that this situation can be turned to advantage for everyone concerned.

Look at the continuum below and mark an x to indicate where you think the training function in your organization stands at the moment. Then date your x; you will find it interesting to revisit this page in months and years to come.

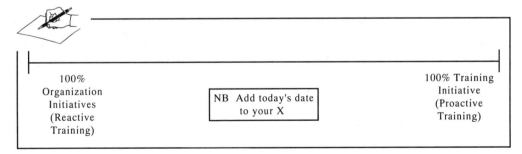

100% Organization Initiatives (Reactive Training)	NB Add today's date to your X	100% Training Initiative (Proactive Training)

Continuous Improvement — A Proactive Role for Training

Finding out about training needs once is not enough to ensure that the training function provides a high quality product. To achieve high quality and a high level of added value, the training function must be continually assessing the changes facing the organization and deciding when and how to respond to those changes.

Think for a moment about changes which have occurred in your organization during the recent past. List three or four of them here and in the column on the right write in the role expected of training.

Recent Changes	*Role(s) Expected of Training*
1	1
2	2
3	3
4	4

In this box below write in what training could have done if it had been given a free rein.

What could training have done?

1.

2.

3.

4.

We cannot comment here on the notes you have made but when we ask this question in workshops the second box usually contains some interesting and exciting possibilities. Here are a few typical, and verbatim, comments:

- '. . . if we'd known three months earlier we could have had the key people ready to start on day one not two weeks later.'

- 'We were told we had to give our people skills training. It was only when we got started that we found out there was a whole new reason for doing what we were doing. So it was attitude development which was actually more important.'

- 'I (lead trainer) didn't have a clue what the big picture was. If I'd known I'd have completely changed the way we chose people for the training **and** the way we delivered it.'

- 'Decisions were made by the senior project team which completely ignored the people side of things and created problems for the training. If took us months to get over those problems which meant the whole project was late starting and went 30% over budget. Next time there will definitely be someone from training in the design team.'

Most of us don't like change. We can talk about the challenge and stimulus of change, but we're really dressing up feelings of fear and insecurity when we do. If that's our reaction when, as trainers, we are agents of change, then we need to be very aware of the doubts, fears, concerns and sometimes blind panic of those to whom change will happen, without their having any control over how or when.

Nevertheless, for the training function, times of change offer a golden opportunity to introduce new ideas and approaches which would have been greeted with overwhelming suspicion when things were relatively calm and static.

What then, does line management in the organization expect from the training function at times of change? Above all it will expect ideas and innovation.

So, in a situation of change, the training function will be expected to come up with some new ideas to make the change easier to cope with. In addition, it is likely to be expected to act as an **agent of change**. This means knowing enough about the people side of the change process to ensure that people have the knowledge, the skills and, perhaps above all, the **confidence** to enter a period of change willingly and with anticipation, rather than in dread.

If the training function is geared to deliver successfully in times of change, it will come to be regarded as capable of moving the organization forward, and of making a strategic contribution.

However, the strategic role can only be effective if you and your training function have access to the right kind of information at the right time.

That means making sure that that the training function has the right kind of access to the right people and the right decision-making forums. Too often we see situations where training needs arising from changes are thought of ten minutes (or less) before a major change goes live. This leaves little room for quality design, and guarantees that training is very badly placed to add value to the organization. It's a classic case of reactive training, and too common by far.

In the box below list the areas within your organization for which you are, or have been, expected to provide training, but where you receive, or have received, too-little or too-late information, then on the right hand side of the box make notes on what you should do to make sure it doesn't happen again.

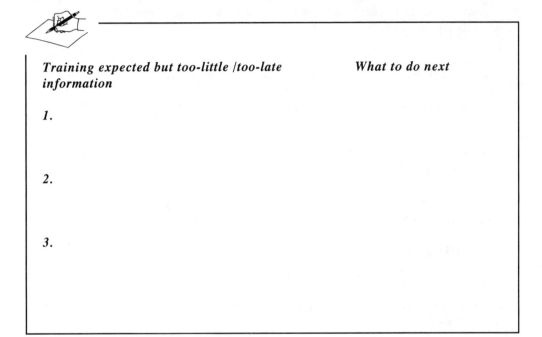

Training expected but too-little /too-late information

What to do next

1.

2.

3.

Again it isn't possible for me to comment in detail on your notes but it is only when the training function has the right kinds of information far enough in advance that it is able to respond quickly, effectively and creatively. In a word to do its job properly — a job which should involve the strategy, tactics and methodology needed to enable people to achieve the organization's purpose, mission, aims and objectives.

Summary

The question 'Why do groups and individuals bother with training' was answered in simple terms: assuming that the training is available, people undertake training because they want to, or they have to.

This state of affairs left you, the trainer, with questions to ask:

- Are your people 'want-to' or 'have-to'?
- Why?
- How can you find out?
- What can you do about it?

You saw that a questionnaire given out to your people would identify whether they 'wanted to' train or 'had to', and that you could also identify whether this was due to:

- irrelevance of training
- inappropriateness of training methods.

You then focused on ways of making your training relevant. The first stage was to ask key questions in the main business activity areas in your organization:

- Finance
- Marketing
- Operations
- Personnel.

Equipped with the answers to these questions, you saw that the next stage was to determine whether a reactive or a proactive stance was going to have the most beneficial effect in your situation.

And now?

You should be aware of why your people and your organization bother with training and what makes your people want to train. You're becoming expert in understanding where your training function fits into your organization.

To conclude and summarize Chapter 2, here is an assignment . . .

Assignment:

Taking the responses to the key questions you asked of the four main business areas in your organization, identify:

- *those areas which need a reactive response from you*
- *those areas which need a proactive response.*

Write them in two lists. From the list of proactive response areas, identify:

- *those which you can address immediately*
- *those which you can only address after a period of consolidation — maybe by concentrating on the reactive areas*
- *how you can ensure that training can be more proactive.*

Promoting Training

The notion of 'promoting' training may be new to you, but it is a vital part of the training function.

There are people within every organization who will be asking whether a training function is necessary at all. Just one step away from this are those who see the point of organized training, but do not see why it can't be bought in all the time from external suppliers like training consultants.

You know why you're there. Presumably you've come through a rigorous interview to get the job; and as you've read Chapters 1 and 2 of this book, you're there to benefit the business by benefiting the people in the business . . . but you **would** say that, wouldn't you? You're protecting your job.

This chapter will show you ways of 'getting the message across' to other people about the key part a well organized training function can play in an organization's success. There are many groups of people in and around an organization whose support you will be relying on for the training function to succeed.

By the time you've read this chapter, you'll know:

- who those people are
- who your competitors are
- how to explain what it is that you do
- how to explain what your training will achieve for others.

Training as a Product

Customers

Seeing training as a product is not the easiest thing to do. If training is a product, then in common with other products in the marketplace, it has to be sold: and that implies not only the existence of customers, but also of customers with money to spend.

So who are the customers for your training?
Write down in this box who you think your customers are. Be specific, use names, groups of names, departments and so on.

There's no way we can comment on what you have written here but in general terms the whole of the organization is your customer. But we asked you to be specific so we have divided customer groups into levels. You should find it useful to discover where your suggested customers come in our 'customer hierarchy' as outlined below.

The Customer Hierarchy

Level 1: Board, senior management
People at level 1 provide the funds for their junior colleagues to spend on training — or on whatever else they feel to be appropriate. Level 1 customers are sometimes referred to as 'sponsors'.

Level 2: Middle management, line management
People at level 2 have the authority to send people for training, set time aside for training, buy in computers, or do whatever else it takes to make this part of the business a success. These people have money, authority and need.

Level 3: Trainees, staff undergoing development
People at level 3 actually use your training by taking what they learn and applying it in their daily routine. They are known as 'end-users'.

Level 4: Peripheral people
There are countless people who benefit from effective training in an organization — its shareholders, its customers, its suppliers — and all the families of the people who work there. Broadly speaking these are 'stakeholders'.

Take our hierarchy and go back to the list you made on the previous page. Beside each customer you've listed write in their level.

Now who are you going to target as you seek to sell your product? The most cost-effective option is the people at level 2. This is where the customers with the money are largely to be found.

Assignment:

From your list on page 59 make a list of people at level 2 in your organization. These are people to whom you could potentially provide training.

Arrange to see each one for a half-hour interview.

Before you conduct the interview, prepare a sheet with these important questions on it (you may think of others too):

- *what benefits would they like to see from training?*
- *what makes them approach you (or anyone else) for training?*
- *who do they approach for training? Is it you? Why (not)?*
- *would they recommend your services to anyone else? Why (not)?*
- *how much time/money/resource can they commit to training?*

True, there are some heart-stopping questions there, and you should be ready for some very frank answers, particularly if you're coming into a situation where training has been neglected for a number of years. But you need honest answers if you are to do your job properly.

To continue, then: when you've got your answers, what do you do when you've compiled your data?

Before you decide, consider the following case study.

Case Study

Sol Gluckmann was appointed training manager at GKD Plastics, an employer of 900 people at three sites in the South West.

He discovered that Liz Anderson from quality supervision has been sending her team to Sol's predecessor for regular training updates for years; the format of the session was well established and Liz's team always went away feeling better able to do their jobs.

Sol also discovered that Max Quigley from design and development hadn't sent any designers for training for years. He just called informal meetings every now and then or organized a 'brown bag lunch' where every designer took a turn in sharing with his or her colleagues an innovation or an item of interest over the lunch-hour.

Sol devoted his efforts to winning over Max Quigley — he even purchased design software for the designers to use if they came to train. He neglected Liz Anderson for six months during his 'Max' campaign.

Max refused to be tempted and Liz took her team elsewhere.

So — to repeat the question: what do you do with the data you've compiled? Write your answer here:

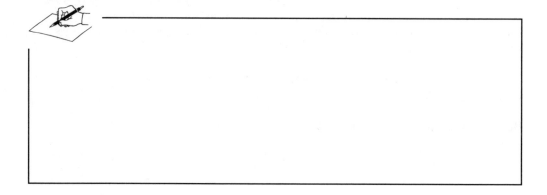

First, you identify your good customers, so that you can **continue** to do something which you know is going well.

Second, you draw up a schedule for keeping in touch with your customers so that you're seeing most often the ones with whom you're most likely to do business.

Product

In most situations regarding training as 'a' product is misleading. In common with most shops, you are probably offering a **range** of products, each one with its unique features.

Assignment:

Draw up a list of all your training programmes and services. Opposite each, write a brief description to include:

- *its content*
- *its length*
- *its style (course, booklet, residential, etc).*

Then asterisk which features makes that particular product unique.

The next stage is to appraise the quality of each product. You must be quite specific about what you mean by 'quality'. We define 'quality' as 'what the customer expects'. Thus the cheapest Yugo and the most expensive Mercedes both represent quality, for a particular customer group with particular needs.

Does your training provision give the customers what they want? We believe you've already got the answers to that question, because you've conducted several inquiries inside the organization already.

Quality — The Materials Themselves

Just as a shopkeeper will go through his or her shelves from time to time to see if there are goods which aren't selling, so you should examine your training provision. Are there courses there which people simply aren't taking up? If so, you have a simple choice: try to sell the course, or scrap it. There is an alternative — just to leave the course available, but put no effort into selling it.

Why do you think we would recommend you not to do the alternative? Write your answer here:

A shopkeeper needs to get maximum benefit from his or her shelves — which means stocking them with saleable items. Your organization — and you as trainer — need to get maximum benefit from the training function. This means keeping only current and relevant courses available.

You should also ask yourself why it is that your training provision isn't 'selling'. If it is due to changes within the business, then it is time for the training to be revised. If there are no changes in that area of the business, then there must be something inherently wrong, either:

- in the way you're selling the product

    or

- in the product itself.

Quality — The Time Factor

Timing is a crucial factor in training because your provision can match the customers' needs exactly, but if it's a day late, or a week late — you could be in trouble.

Think of one way of training where timing is particularly critical.

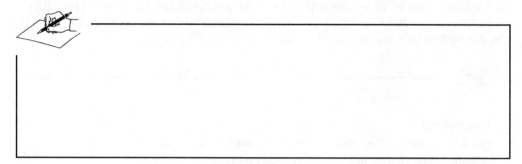

We thought of computer systems training. If your organization is due to change from one system to another on, say, November 30 and your training isn't ready until December 4 — the costs to the business could potentially be huge.

Quality — Gaps in your Provision

There are occasions when it is useful to send your people on outside courses, or to buy training in — because sometimes an outsider's perspective is essential. But there are times when training should be provided in-house but isn't because the training function hasn't the resources or the expertise.

If you are buying in training for the second of these reasons the chances are that your overall quality will be perceived as low, and you can't expect people to go on buying it.

Quality — Bread and Butter Products vs New Products

Marketing wisdom has it that all products have three stages in their lives:

- growth
- maturity
- decline.

New products reach their maximum sales figures quickly (growth), hold high levels for a while — maybe years (maturity), and then gradually fall away (decline). It is the success of products in their maturity phase which allows the business to invest in new products which will eventually replace the declining ones.

Assignment:

Against each of the 'products' you offer, pencil in the letter G, M or D to indicate whether that product is in growth, maturity or decline.

This will help you to see which 'products' to keep going while you develop new ones. You will probably find that your bread-and-butter products all fall into the M category.

Training as a Product — the Competitors

Given that the people in level 2 of the customer hierarchy may have control of an overall (finite) budget, 'competition' can arise from areas other than training. The warehousing department may spend their money on facilitization and completely neglect the training implications. Other than expanding on the benefits of training to budget holders, there is little you can do in this situation.

More within your power are your competitors in the training field.

Answer the questions below in the space provided.

1. **How do you find out who your competitors are?**

2. **What do you need to know about the competition?**

You can find out who your competitors are by asking your customers:

- who has approached them offering training
- who they (the customers) have approached enquiring about training.

You need to know a number of things quite urgently, and you should ask your customers:

- for what products do they actually prefer the competition? Why?
- for what products do they positively prefer you? — and why?

Opportunities and Threats

The answers you receive to the above questions may appear quite threatening. To take an extreme example, it is possible that all your customers prefer your competitors because their product is more objectives-driven and up-to-date than yours. But having gathered this information you are in a very strong position to do something about it.

Training? What Training?

You may find that the potential customers in your business are simply unaware of the training you provide, or the way in which you can design and deliver something to meet their needs.

There are two possible — and very different — reasons for this, but there is one solution. We'll deal with this straight away.

There are two reasons why managers and other potential customers don't know what training can achieve. Either:

- training is so ineffectual that they don't notice its input, or
- training is so effectual that it's achieving everything with no fuss.

Ineffectual Training

If a manager sends a team to be trained and they come back none the wiser, he or she will assume that the training might as well not have taken place and will seek another training provider or do without.

Effectual Training

Below is a list of three automobile parts. Which one has most in common with an effectual training function — and why?

a.   the engine

b.   the wheels

c.   the lubricant.

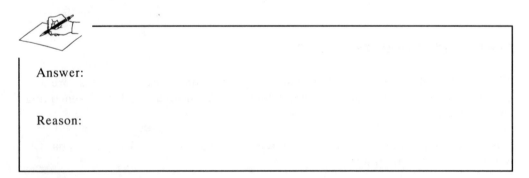

Answer:

Reason:

We chose the **lubricant**. This is because a lubricant allows the important parts of the vehicle to perform their tasks efficiently and effectively without being especially visible or drawing attention to itself.

The measure of a successful training function is that the organization it serves does well. Human nature dictates that the producers within an organization will tend to congratulate themselves for this state of affairs. The contribution of training may be overlooked.

The solution from your point of view is to **promote training**.

There are three basic steps involved in promoting training.

Step 1 — List the benefits to your organization created by each element within your training provision. You will have to list the elements one by one, and opposite each compile a list of benefits: the benefits you read about in Chapter 1 will be a useful starting point.

Step 2 — Compile a list of the people and groups of people within your organization who will benefit from your training provision. As a rough guide, your list will include:

- customers
- end-users
- sponsors
- the whole organization.

You will need to be more specific, as you'll see.

Step 3 — Advertise the benefits appropriately.

Use the space below to show how you would advertise training to *three* of the people and groups listed in Step 2 (above).

Person/group	Advertise method

Here are some suggestions.

Person/group	Advertizing method
New employees	Video
	Introductory 'Welcome' pamphlet
Board/senior managers	Presentation
	Reports
Customers	Visits
	Newsletter

Your list will almost certainly be different from ours, but you should at least be aware of the need to be specific when targeting your advertisements, and of the range of possibilities which exists.

Summary

In this chapter you have seen that one of the keys to the success of the training function is to promote training. Training, if not promoted will appear invisible or will be underrated. Promoting training is achieved:

- first, by treating training as a product
- second, by identifying people within your organization as 'customers' for that product. 'Customers' — a broad term — includes sponsors, purchasers, end-users and stakeholders
- third, by instigating a three-stage promotion plan, involving identification of the benefits of training, describing the way those benefits are felt by different people, and advertising the benefits appropriately.

As usual, we will conclude this chapter with an assignment for you to put some of the ideas you've been reading about into practice.

Assignment:

1. *Identify by name the main sponsors and purchasers of training in your organization.*

2. *Prioritize them according to the amount of training you have provided for them over the last two years.*

3. *List the training 'products' which you provide.*

4. *Prioritize them according to their popularity over the last two years.*

5. *Match up your products as follows:*

    a.   successful established products — good established customers

    b.   successful established products — irregular or new customers

    c.   less successful or new products — good established customers

6. *Prepare a promotion plan which sells the benefits of each piece of training to the people who will buy it, working your way down the list above from a. to c.*

7. *Implement the plan!*

**The South East Essex
College of Arts & Technology**
Carnarvon Road, South̶ ̶ ̶ ̶ ̶ ̶ ̶ ̶ ̶ ̶ SS2 6LS
Phone 0702 220400 Fax 0702 432320 Minicom 0702 220642

The Training Function —
What is it?

We have not yet properly addressed the question of what the training function is and what it actually does.

True, there has been plenty of discussion about what the training function can achieve and how it can benefit people — and so benefit the organization. But . . . as for what it **is** and **does** . . . you'll need to have the answer to those questions clear, because they are the standard, challenging, put-you-down questions uttered by managers and staff in areas of the business which actually produce things.

By the time you've finished this chapter, you will:

- have an appropriate, working definition of the training function for use in your organization
- be able to explain what it is that you do
  — in broad terms
  — in specific terms.

You will also be well on the way to a complete understanding of the training function.

Alignment

We mentioned in Chapter 3 that the training function is like a lubricant which allows the different parts of the whole to work properly.

Another way of expanding this is to say the training function has a relationship with its host organization. For that relationship to be mutually beneficial, it must be close — not to say intimate.

But not all relationships between the training function and its host organizations are intimate. Look at this extreme example.

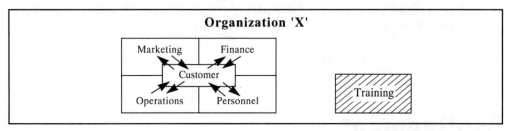

Of course, it's a caricature — but it represents a typical situation in what is otherwise an effective customer-orientated, marketing-led organization. Training has been left to focus on nothing more profitable than its own navel. In a situation like this, training will be seen as cost-centre with no contribution to make. Training will not be involved in the corporate planning process and will therefore be left with whatever resources the organization is grudgingly prepared to spare it.

If you analyse your situation and find your training function in a remote relationship like this, you'll need to realign it, about which more later.

A more satisfactory relationship is like this.

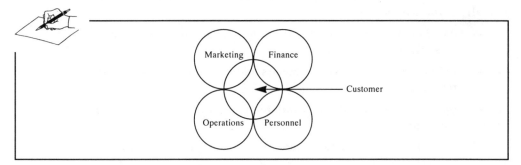

Shade in where training will appear in this diagram.

Did you shade in the interfaces between the departments? Good — because training can and should work in areas where two or more functions are in close co-operation.

Did you shade in the whole thing? Even better — because training has no existence except in its relationship with the other functions. That, in a nutshell, is what the training function **is** — or should be. The training function should provide the people development support it and every other part of the organization needs to achieve its aims and objectives.

Realignment

If your training function is remote from the other parts of the organization, you must realign it. Realignment is not a quick job; a timescale of two years is common in larger organizations. Realignment means, simply, putting training into its proper relationship with the host organization. However, a statement of policy — for example 'from today the training function will become an integral part of all other functions' — isn't going to convince anyone.

You have to **do** something. The purpose of this book is to explain what the training function is, so it would be inappropriate to go into detail about how to realign a remote training function into a more central position. Suffice it to say that in order to realign, you will need to:

- come up with ideas to make training relevant or let everyone know it **is** relevant

- promote your ideas with sponsors and customers so as to acquire resources

- plan a strategy within the available resources of money, equipment and people

- concentrate on the areas where there is the greatest likelihood of success.

What the Training Function Does

The role of the training function can be divided into two:

- finding things out
- putting things into action in the area of people development to achieve the mission and purpose of the organization. Where there is only one person co-ordinating the training then that person's time should be divided fairly evenly between these two broad areas. Where a team is involved in training the tasks can be shared.

Finding Things Out

What sort of things do you feel the training function would spend time trying to find out? Some of your ideas may come from earlier sections of this book. Others may well be new. Write your list here:

From inside the organization

From outside the organization

Check how your list matches ours:

a.   Inside the organization

1.   How can you start to promote training? (See Chapter 3)

2.   What do the people here need or expect from training? (See Chapter 2)

3.   Why does this organization need training? (See Chapter 1)

4.   What is the culture of this organization?

5.   How important is training in the different areas of the business to the survival and prosperity of the organization as a whole?

This fifth point is crucial to the success of the training function, because unless its training provision mirrors the training needs of the organization in terms of priority, then it stands to lose credibility — and ultimately the whole organization will suffer.

b.   Outside the organization

1.   What is new in the way of training approaches and methodology?

2.   Who else is facing the same problems as you and what are they doing about them?

3.   What future developments are starting out in training?

4.   Which are relevant to you and how can you begin to prepare to introduce them?

A simple way to set about these investigations is to subscribe to magazines which specialize in your particular industrial or market sector.

The importance of training in the different areas can be gauged by measuring the training gap.

The Training Gap

In its simplest terms, the difference between a person's actual job performance and their required job performance is called 'the training gap'.

Finding out about job performance involves analysing:

- job content

  and

- standards.

Of course you will need to be specific about both points. Being specific about job content will mean that you have to be where the work is done. Actually being there and gaining the trust of the people in your organization will reinforce the intimate relationship. You can discuss things with the employees and their managers.

Specific details about performance standards will be found in performance agreements, appraisal assessments, the organization's objectives and, as above, in conversation with the people who do the job.

The Magnitude of the Training Gap

In an organization there may be many training gaps. There are two factors which can make a training gap a high priority. See if you can identify them here.

-

-

The two factors which influence the prioritizing of a training gap are:

- the immediate importance of the task to the organization's survival and prosperity
- the numbers of people involved.

For example, your organization depends on only two salespeople for its sales, neither of whom is up to the required performance. So their significance is high and their training is a high priority. You also have a large team of junior clerical staff, none of whom are up to standard. They may not have immediate significance for survival but by force of numbers provide a high risk of error-related problems occurring.

In an ideal world, every worker would be trained to perfection in all the skills of their job. In reality, we have limited resources and need to concentrate them in areas of greatest need. One way to focus our attention is by considering the cost which the organization incurs by leaving a training gap unfilled. This cost may be in terms of lost turnover, customer complaints, rectification, or reduced efficiency.

By going through these three stages you will have established the nature of the training need and whether it is important enough to require action:

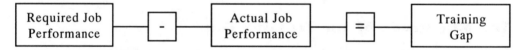

When you have found out information from:

- inside the organization

  and

- outside the organization

then the remaining activity of the training function is **to put things into action**.

Putting Things into Action

Putting things into action is itself a two-stage process:

- first, there comes a planning stage in response to the information you have been gathering
- second, comes the implementation of training.

The Planning Stage

A lot of information you have been gathering from within the organization will come together to paint a picture of:

- the training need
- the people
- the organization.

The Training Need

Training needs are traditionally divided into three areas.

Write down in this box what you think the three broad areas actually are.

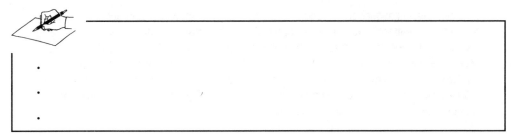

-
-
-

Traditionally, training is divided into:

- knowledge
- skills
- attitudes.

In broad terms, the training you implement to meet each of those needs will be different. Gaps in the knowledge can, for example, be bridged in courses away from the workplace. Gaps in skills need to be addressed at the time and place where the skill is actually used. You can see that this planning stage is absolutely crucial.

The People

Key people-issues are less complicated than you might at first think. Your ultimate course of action will be determined more by:

- how many people are involved
- where these people are located

than by:

- learning style and preferences.

Case Study

A chain of retail pharmacists needed their staff to be more knowledgeable about the reasons why various treatments were or were not effective. Their staff were distributed in teams of ten or less nationwide, and they had bad experiences of poor quality open learning. The trainer decided that on balance, open learning was the only viable route to follow, as conferences would have been less effective, even though conferences were their preferred learning method. A high quality open learning scheme was prepared. It was then launched and promoted widely and ended up as a success.

The Organization

To maximize the chance of success you invariably have to work within the parameters of what is culturally acceptable within your organization.

Case Study

The trainers in a large financial institution perceived a need for communication training to overcome barriers which existed between different levels of the hierarchy. To achieve this they ran group courses with representatives in each group from all levels of management. The result? Often senior managers didn't turn up (they were too busy doing their real work!) — or, if they did turn up, they so intimidated everyone that the initiative failed. The biggest mistake any trainer can make is to force an unsuitable training approach on an unwilling organization.

Implementation

Implementing training is a large subject and in terms of this book, to 'understand the training function' you need only to be aware that:

- implementation is an issue
- there are many types of training available
- for every type of training there are stages you must work through: before, during and after the training
- making things run smoothly will enhance your reputation.

How many different types of training can you think of? List them here:

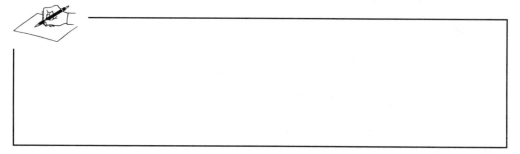

We have identified six — you may have come up with more:

- group training
- side-by-side training
- text-based open learning
- technology-based training
- discovery learning
- multi-media.

It's possible that there will be a fair degree of overlap between your answers and ours, although you may have used different words.

For each of the training methods, there will be stages of:

- preparation
- execution
- evaluation

all of which are essential if you are to implement training successfully.

List the areas of activity in which a training function could be involved before, during and after a group training session — and don't forget peripheral, supporting tasks.

Before:
- clear and comprehensive joining instructions
- time to prepare (pre-course sending of case studies, etc)
- accurate and sympathetic briefing
- course reception and welcome.

During:
- course delivery
- administrative support
- timekeeping
- review
- feedback.

After:
- full and informed debriefing
- follow-up action plan
- time to implement
- regular reviews
- evaluating the effectiveness and the training. The final 'toolkit' in this series deals with evaluation issues in some detail.

However, no training course or any other training method will work in a vacuum. Implementation means ensuring that there is a comprehensive and reliable mechanism all around it.

The End of the Road?

The training function which exists in a close relationship with other functions, which has obtained all the data it needs from inside and outside the organization and which has implemented courses accordingly need not fear that they have trained themselves out of a job.

There are two reasons why training will continue. Identify the reasons why training is ongoing and write them down in this box.

:
:

First, there will always be new people joining the organization. Second, people who are trained well will find themselves:

· ready to take on more responsibility

· expecting to contribute more to the organization

· motivated to learn and explore.

All of these need more training. The one aspect of organizational activity we can all guarantee will continue and possibly at a faster pace then it has done during the last decade, is CHANGE. And successful change takes place when people receive timely and relevant support. The training function has a major role to play in providing that support. People have said that training is cyclical. It isn't. It's an upward spiral of ever increasing expectations and challenges. Whatever else it may be, a trainer's life is never boring!

Summary

Chapter 4 set out to describe what the training function is and what the training function does.

The training function exists only in its relationship with other functions of the host organization; its ultimate success is measurable only in terms of their ultimate success. The training function does two things:

· it obtains information

· it implements training.

Obtaining information requires questions to be asked inside and outside the organization — so that you know what areas need training and how best to provide it. Implementing training requires not only course delivery, but also a detailed scheme of support before, during and after delivery.

Finally, you saw that training as a task is never completed. Good training causes more training — at a higher level — to be needed, and so on in an ever-upward spiral.

The Trainer's Role

This last chapter is designed around a set of questions which will help you to focus your mind on what your position is within the training function.

By the time you have finished this chapter, you will be able to:

- identify six areas of the trainer's role within the training function
- identify specific tasks which need to be carried out within each of the six areas
- prepare an action plan which will enable you to address priority tasks within your role in the training function.

Six Areas

It's not unusual for new trainers or those people with limited experience of the training function to be surprised at the range of work which takes place within it.

By taking the entire range of activities and dividing them into six identifiable areas, you will find it easier to come to grips with the whole.

The following three pages contain lists of tasks commonly associated with different areas of the training function. After each is a box for you to tick yes or no to show whether you are involved in that task or not.

Completing this exercise will enable you to:

· identify those areas in which you are involved

· identify those areas in which you need to become involved if the training function is to play its full part in your organization.

Ultimately, this may lead to your achieving greater job satisfaction, as you identify exactly what it is you need to do.

To help you with the planning of the inevitable task-list which will fall out of the following activity, there is an action-planning matrix on page 91.

Area 1: The Management of Training

	Yes	No
a. Representing the training function at interdepartmental meetings.	O	O
b. Gathering **and using** information about developments in finance, marketing, operations and personnel in your organization.	O	O
c. Gathering **and using** information about developments in training outside your organization.	O	O
d. Analysing **and responding** to people's feelings about training inside your organization.	O	O
e. Preparing financial plans for the training function.	O	O
f. Submitting resource requirements for training.	O	O
g. Promoting training.	O	O

Area 2: Encouraging Learning

		Yes	No
a.	Designing training material — courses, packages, events.	O	O
b.	Influencing who gets what form of training within the organization.	O	O
c.	Commissioning training material from outside the organization.	O	O
d.	Having a say in the briefing of trainees.	O	O
e.	Getting involved in monitoring training.	O	O
f.	Having anything to do with line managers supporting trainees.	O	O

Area 3: Identifying and Analysing Training Needs

		Yes	No
a.	Helping establish performance standards.	O	O
b.	Designing measures of performance in the training environment.	O	O
c.	Contributing to performance measurement in the workplace.	O	O
d.	Setting training priorities.	O	O
e.	Helping identify causes of under-performance.	O	O
f.	Negotiating training and other responses with line management.	O	O

Area 4: Selecting Training Methods

		Yes	No
a.	Making any use of the knowledge — skills — attitudes breakdown of training needs.	O	O
b.	Involving yourself in analysing potential trainees by number, location, education and background and preferred learning style.	O	O
c.	Contributing to identifying training methods acceptable to your organization.	O	O
d.	Influencing the training methodology (courses, manuals, hardware, software, equipment) used in your organization.	O	O
e.	Helping determine who gets what form of training in the organization.	O	O
f.	Having complete responsibility for one type of trainee (apprentices, new starters, clerical staff, managers)	O	O

Area 5: Implementing Training

		Yes	No
a.	Side-by-side training.	O	O
b.	Group instruction.	O	O
c.	Experimental learning.	O	O
d.	Residential courses.	O	O
e.	Text-based open learning.	O	O
f.	Technology based training (also know as 'computer - aided learning').	O	O
g.	Interactive video.	O	O
h.	CDi.	O	O

Area 6: Evaluating Training

		Yes	No
a.	Validating training. Checking trainees can meet learning objectives after training.	O	O
b.	Comparing pre- and post-training performance.	O	O
c.	Designing end-of-course questionnaires.	O	O
d.	Carrying out post-training follow-up.	O	O
e.	Checking performance back in the workplace.	O	O
f.	Holding training reviews with line managers.	O	O
g.	Influencing the objectives of the training function.	O	O

The Training Function and Where You Fit In

For your final activity in this book we ask you to transfer your ticks and crosses from the last three pages to the matrix on page 91.

After each area, there is space for you to write down the **action** which your profile of ticks and crosses suggests to you. The action may be — nothing; leave it alone, you've got it under control. Or the action may be — get help; ask for resources of people and training for yourself.

Only you can tell — it's within your organization where your understanding of the training function will actually account for something.

Conclusion

From a starting point of not being sure of what your training function is or does, you've seen:

- the benefits your organization is looking for
- what your people need to make them want to train
- why promoting training is so important
- what the training function comprises
- what your relationship is to the training function.

Now you understand the training function well enough to decide what to do to make it work in your organization. We'll leave you with the matrix and your action plan. We wish you happy training.

Area	Task								Action
	a	b	c	d	e	f	g	h	
1									
2									
3									
4									
5									
6									